Ben Dinat!

Authentic Family Recipes from the Island of Mallorca

Copyright 2016 Taylor Press

Photography by D. Charles Photography

Taylor Press/Ben Dinat! - Family Recipes from the Island of Mallorca

PO Box 357, 612-500 Country Hills Blvd NE

Calgary, Alberta T3K 5K3

ISBN: 978-0-9952621-0-2

Library of Parliament Cataloging-in-Publication Data

Printed in Canada

First Printing

0 40232 49457 4

First Edition

Ben Dinat!

Authentic Family Recipes from the Island of Mallorca

The ingredients are simple and largely accepted
worldwide, no surprises or hard-to-come by ingredients.

These authentic Mallorquin family recipes are unique in
their development, rich in their ancestry and appreciated
for their romantic character . . . delightful, yet simple.

I offer this to anyone with a special interest
in our authentic Mallorquin family recipes.

My objective is to give you an uncomplicated,
easy-to-read and understand recipe book with
clear instructions and lists of ingredients that are
readily accessible and cost-effective.

Legend has it that after the battle for the conquest of Mallorca on September 12, 1229, a famished King James I of Aragon came upon a tent with one of his lieutenants near the Port of Mallorca. In the tent, a meal was being prepared by Oliver de Térmens.[1] After eating this simple dinner of bread with garlic to their satisfaction, the king declared:

Ben Dínat!
" We have eaten well!"

---

[1] Found in the *Llibre dels Feits del Rei En Jaume* Chronicle.

Foreword

I was born in Palma de Mallorca, Spain. My family has been in the hospitality industry for more than ten decades. On my last trip to my birth place, I noticed that although many cook books have been published as "Spanish cook books", few featured traditional and authentic recipes exclusively from the island of Mallorca. This was a turning point. After seeking my mother's culinary opinion and receiving her blessing, I embarked on what I hope will elicit *Ben Dinat!* from all who enjoy this book.

Initially I asked, "How could I write a cook book with authentic Mallorquin family recipes? And who would be interested?" Most cook books are written by food enthusiasts and celebrities, well recognized around the world. My desire and mission is to share traditional Mallorquin recipes that have been around for centuries, enjoyed by families like mine.

I offer this to anyone with a special interest in authentic "Receptes Mallorquinas de la meva familia". My objective is to give you an uncomplicated, easy-to-read and understand recipe book with clear instructions and lists of ingredients that are readily accessible and cost-effective. I hope that for any visitor to Mallorca, or for those interested in old fashioned Mallorquin cooking, this cook book will be a small piece of the Island's history that can serve to bring back or create happy memories of a place so many of us love.

Es meu cô no me basta per li di adiós — "My heart will not let me say farewell"

-- Meric Taylor

Contents

Sopes i enseladas
Soups and Salads

Plats de Peix i Marisc
Fish and Seafood

Bacalla amb Espinacs i Pasas *Cod Fish with Spinach and Raisins*	9
Caldereta de Peix *Fish Soup Cauldron*	10
Escabeche *Trout Marinated in Olive Oil and Garlic*	11
Gambes a l'All *Sautéed Prawns in Garlic*	12
Paella de Marisc *Seafood Paella*	13
Rap amb Pèsols *Brandy-infused Monk Fish with Peas*	14

Plats de Verdura
Vegetable Entrées

Coca de Pebres Torrats *Mallorquin Flatbread with Roasted Peppers*	15
Llenties Mallorquines *Mallorquin Lentils with Zucchini*	16
Sopes Mallorquines *Traditional Mallorquin Vegetable 'Greixonera'*	17
Coca de Verdura *Mallorquin Flatbread with Vegetables and Olive Oil*	18
Tumbet Mallorqui *Aubergine and Zucchini Casserole*	19
Flam d'Espinacs *Mallorquin Spinach and Cheese Custard*	20
Truita de Patata *Egg and Potato Torte*	22

Plats de Carn
Meat Entrées

Arròs Brut *'Dirty' Rice*	25
Choriz i Ciurons *Chorizo with Chickpeas*	26
Frit Mallorqui *Mallorquin Fritata*	27
Paella *Traditional Saffron Rice with Meat*	28
Pilotes Mallorquinas en Vi Blanc *Mallorquin Meatballs in White Wine Sauce*	29
Pollestre al Jerez *Sherry-infused Chicken in Cream Sauce*	30

Galletes, Cocas i Postres
Cookies, Cakes and Puddings

Coca d'Albercocs *Apricot Cake*	33
Coca de Fruita i Coñac *Cognac Fruit Bread*	34
Coca amb Ron Mallorqui *Mallorquin Rum Cake*	35
Gató Mallorqui *Mallorquin Almond Cake*	36
Galletes de Maizena *Sweet Cookies*	38
Greixonera d'Ensaïmada *Ensaïmada Bread Pudding*	39
Postre de Poma amb Ron *Apple Rum Cake*	40

Sangria Mallorquina   42

Country Bread with Olive Oil   4

Sopes i enseladas
Soups and Salads

All i Oli
Mallorquin Garlic Mayonnaise

My great grandmother used ¼ cup fresh parsley not only as a garnish but to add additional flavour.

Preparation time: 20 minutes

Ingredients

1 garlic clove, peeled
1 large egg yolk
1 teaspoon Dijon mustard
1 ¼ cup extra virgin olive oil
1 ¼ cup olive oil
1 teaspoon salt
Lemon juice to taste
Fresh country bread

Method

In a pestle and mortar, mash up the garlic with 1 teaspoon of salt

Place the egg yolk and mustard in a bowl and whisk together, then start to add your oils a little bit at a time

Once half of the oils are blended, start to add the rest in larger amounts

The mixture will slowly start to thicken. When it does, add the lemon juice

Once all the oils have been used, add the mashed garlic

Serve with fresh country bread

Makes ½ cup mayonnaise

Enselada de Ciurons i Atun
Chickpea and Tuna Salad

An easy recipe ... a few healthy ingredients mixed together and you have a superb salad.

Preparation time: 20 minutes

Ingredients

1 can of chickpeas, drained
¼ sweet onion, sliced thin
1 can of tuna in olive oil (not water)
¼ cup olive oil
½ teaspoon paprika
Salt and pepper to taste

Method

Mix all ingredients together in a large bowl
Place the bowl in the fridge until ready to serve
Serve cold with fresh country bread or hardy crackers

Serves 4

Gaspatxo Mallorquin
Chilled Gaspatcho Vegetable Soup

A refreshing summer soup, loaded with fresh, crunchy vegetables and herbs. Tomatoes, cucumber, pepper and onion give it a delightful colour. The flavour of Gaspatxo Mallorquin improves if allowed to chill overnight.

Preparation time: 30 minutes

Ingredients

6 TBSP olive oil
1 teaspoon tarragon
3 large tomatoes
2 garlic cloves
1 small sweet onion
1 small cucumber
1 red bell pepper
2 TBSP red vinegar
½ cup bread crumbs (no crusts)
2 TBSP fresh chopped parsley (for garnishing)

Method

Peel tomatoes, cucumber, onions and garlic

Cut into cubes

Place all ingredients (except bread crumbs and parsley) in a blender

Blend until semi-pureed or to consistency desired

Chill in refrigerator until ready to serve

Serve in soup bowls with bread crumbs and parsley as garnish

Serves 4

Pa Amb Oli
Country Bread with Olive Oil

Preparation time: 30 minutes

Ingredients

4 thick slices fresh country bread
2 garlic cloves
2 TBSP olive oil (per bread slice or to taste preference)
2 medium tomatoes (ripe)
Olives
Salt to taste

Method

Lightly toast 2 slices per person of brown country bread
(thick sliced), then rub over with a clove of garlic

Drizzle over a small amount of olive oil, rub with a half
tomato and sprinkle salt to taste

Serve with garnish of olives

Serves 2

Pancuit
Mallorquin Garlic Soup

Preparation time: 20 minutes

Ingredients

8 garlic cloves sliced
1 teaspoons paprika
4 TBSP olive oil
1 ½ litres hot water
½ loaf day-old bread, cubed into 2" x 2" pieces (include the crusts)
3 slices of "Jamon Serrano' or Prosciutto ham, finely diced
3 eggs, beaten
1 bay leaf
Salt and pepper

Method

In a pan, sauté paprika in olive oil on low heat for one minute

Add the sliced garlic, and sauté for 3 minutes, do not brown

Add ham, sauté for 2 minutes

Add hot water, bring almost to a boil, then back down to a simmer

Add day old bread (including crusts!) and bay leaf

Cook for 30 minutes on low heat (don't boil)

Add more water if the soup becomes too thick

Add eggs, stir and serve

Salt and pepper to taste

Serves 4

Trampó
Mallorquin Country Salad

Preparation time: 20 minutes

Ingredients

1 white onion	2 garlic cloves	4 red peppers
4 large firm tomatoes	1 TBSP red vinegar	3 TBSP olive oil
3/4 cup olives	2 TBSP capers (optional)	Salt to taste

Method

Thinly slice white onions and garlic

Slice red peppers and tomatoes

Toss all ingredients in a bowl

Chill and serve 20 minutes later

Serves 6

Pebres Vermells Torrats
Roasted Red Peppers

Preparation time: **45 minutes**

Ingredients

4 large, red bell peppers, roasted*
2 garlic cloves, roasted
Balsamic or red wine vinegar
Fresh basil
Salt and pepper to taste
Olive oil
*for roasting, brush entire surface of peppers and cloves
with olive oil then place peppers and garlic cloves in oven
for 30 minutes at 375 F.

Method

Preheat oven to 375° F.

Roast the peppers in oven. Remove the skin, the stem,
core and seeds when cooled. Cut into 2" strips lengthwise.
Place the pepper strips in a bowl

Sprinkle with the remaining ingredients

Oil and vinegar to taste

Serve at room temperature

Accompany the peppers with fresh bread

Serves 4

8

Plats de Peix i Marisc

Fish and Seafood

Bacallà Amb Espinacs i Pasas
Cod Fish with Spinach and Raisins

Preparation time: 20 minutes
Cooking time: 40 minutes

Ingredients

1 ½ lbs Cod fish (boneless)   2 spinach bunches
1 fresh parsley bunches   1 medium sweet onions
2 medium-sized tomatoes   4 garlic cloves
¾ cup raisins   1 cup breadcrumbs
1 TBSP Paprika   4 oz olive oil
6 oz water

Method

Preheat oven to 325° F.

Finely chop the onions and place them at the bottom of the glass oven-proof dish

Place the cod fillets on top of the onions. Add 6 oz water

Wash the spinach and parsley and cut into small pieces

Slice the garlic cloves into medium-sized slices

Place the spinach, parsley, garlic, paprika and raisins over the cod fillets

Slice the tomatoes and place over spinach, parsley, garlic and raisins (as above)

Cover with breadcrumbs

Evenly pour olive oil over the breadcrumbs and bake

Bake for 40 minutes

Serves 4

Caldereta de Peix
Mallorquin Fish Soup

Caldereta de Peix is a very popular Mallorquin dish. It is served in a 'greixonera' or 'clay casserole dish' and brought to the table piping hot.

Preparation time:	30 minutes
Cooking time:	10 minutes
Baking time:	10 minutes

Ingredients

2 lbs white flesh fish (Monk fish is great for this recipe, however if you use Cod instead, omit the salt)
4 medium potatoes (cubed)
2 large fresh tomatoes (diced)
1 hot chili pepper (seeded and chopped)
4 dried hot red peppers (capsicums) (seeded and chopped)

2 garlic cloves	3 TBSP pine nuts	4 oz olive oil
2 cups water	2 cups fish stock	Fresh parsley

Method

Preheat oven to 350° F.

Sauté potatoes in olive oil and chili until potatoes are brown and crispy but not completely cooked

In a mortar or food processor, grind pine nuts, garlic, red peppers (capsicums) and tomatoes

Add to potatoes and simmer for a few minutes, then add fish and the fish stock, simmer for ten minutes

Add water and season

Transfer to individual 'greixoneras' or one large 'greixonera' or a 'clay casserole dish' and place in hot oven for 10 minutes until the sauce thickens. Garnsish with fresh parsley

Serve hot with lots of country bread

Serves 6

Escabeche
Marinated Trout in Olive Oil and Garlic

Preparation time: 45 minutes
Cooking time: 10 minutes

Ingredients

1 lb fish fillets* (de-boned), cut into 2-3 inch pieces
4 cooked tomatoes (or 1 can tomato paste)
6 garlic cloves peeled and thinly sliced

1 large white onion, sliced	1 cup red wine
½ cup red wine vinegar	½ cup Balsamic vinegar
¼ cup olive oil	1 teaspoon coriander seeds
2 TBSP olive oil	1 TBSP paprika
1 TBSP dried oregano leaves	2 TBSP salt
4 bay leaves	1 teaspoon black peppercorns
½ teaspoon cumin seeds	1 teaspoon dried thyme leaves

* Trout and Mackerel are best for this recipe

Method

In a frying pan, add 2 TBSP olive oil, sear the fish (turning fish over once so that both sides are seared). Once the fish is golden brown on both sides, add the garlic, sliced onion and paprika (do not overcook). Turn heat off and transfer to a serving plate, a 'greixonera' or 'clay casserole dish'. Set aside

In a clean pan, place the vinegars, 1/4 cup olive oil, red wine, tomatoes (or tomato paste) and all other ingredients and heat on a low setting for about 10 minutes

Set aside and allow to cool at room temperature for about 15 minutes, then place over the fried fish

Cover and place the fish in the refrigerator overnight to be safe — and then serve cold the next day

Serves 4

Gambes a l'All
Sautéed Prawns in Garlic

Preparation time: 15 minutes
Cooking time: 5 minutes

Ingredients

2 lbs fresh prawns (peeled)
4 garlic cloves (sliced)
2 red chillies (chopped and de-seeded)
½ cup white wine
4 TBSP olive oil
1 fresh lemon
½ cup fresh parsley
Salt and pepper

Method

Wash and peel prawns. Set aside.

In a 'greixonera' or 'clay casserole dish' (or large frying pan), heat the olive oil then add the garlic cloves and red chilies. Cook until golden brown, then add the prawns

Cook the prawns for about 5 minutes or until the prawns turn pink

Add the white wine, salt and pepper to taste and simmer for a few more minutes

Squeeze a fresh lemon over the prawns and garnish with fresh parsley

Serve hot on a bed of lettuce sprinkled with pine nuts or sesame seeds or with fresh country bread

Serves 4

Paella de Marisc
Seafood Paella

Preparation time:	20 minutes
Cooking time:	40 minutes

Ingredients

2 medium pork chops (cut in small cubes)
6 oz beef steak (cut in small cubes)
12 medium sized fresh shrimp (peeled and uncooked)
2 medium sized calamari (thawed calamari rings may be used if fresh is not available)

1 small onion (chopped)	2 medium tomatoes (chopped)
1 red pepper (roasted)	5 TBSP olive oil
2 TBSP saffron powder	Salt and pepper
1 ¼ cup short-grain rice	2 ½ cups water

Clams and mussels may be added.

Method

In a 'paellera' or large shallow frying pan, sauté the onion with the olive oil until golden brown, then add the meat

Continue cooking until the meat is seared on all sides

Add tomatoes, shrimps and calamari, cook on medium heat for 15 minutes

Add water, saffron powder and salt and pepper. Bring to a gentle boil

Add rice to the boiling water stirring once or twice only thus allowing the rice to proportionally settle

Place the roasted peppers on top of the rice (see page 6 for roasting instructions)

Cook for 15 minutes. Add additional water if necessary. Remove from heat and allow rice to settle for 5-6 minutes before serving

Serves 4

Rap amb Pèsols
Monk Fish with Brandy

Monk Fish are ugly, weird-looking fish, however, when they are cooked properly, they have a sweet and mild taste. You would not guess that something so good came from something so ugly. Great with onions and garlic!

Preparation time:	**20 minutes**
Cooking time:	**30 minutes**

Ingredients

2 - 7 oz Monk Fish filets (de-boned)
1 white onion (thinly sliced)
2 garlic cloves (thinly sliced)
2 TBSP olive oil
2 TBSP Brandy
1 cup water
1 cup peas (drained)
1 teaspoon paprika
Salt and pepper

Method

In a pan with 2 TBSP olive oil, sauté the Monk Fish turning over once until golden brown

Place on a dish and set aside

In the same pan, sauté the onion with the garlic cloves and paprika

Add the water, brandy and peas

Allow to come to a gentle boil

Cover and simmer for 30 minutes

Salt and pepper to taste

Serves 4

Plats de Verdura

Vegetable Entrées

Coca de Pebres Torrats
Mallorquin Flatbread with Roasted Red Peppers

Preparation time: 30 minutes
Baking time: 30 minutes (for peppers)
                         30 minutes (for flatbread)

Ingredients for Pastry
(You can substitute home made pastry with store-bought pizza dough)

2 ¼ cup white flour	1 TBSP yeast	3 ½ oz olive oil
3 ½ oz lukewarm water	Pinch of salt	

Method

Dissolve the yeast with a little lukewarm water in a bowl; add the oil, rest of water and the salt. Mix in the flour a little at a time and knead as though making bread. Leave to rise covered with a clean cloth, about 1 hour in a warm place.

Ingredients for Toppings

2 large red peppers	1 small sweet onion	4 garlic cloves
4 TBSP olive oil	Salt and pepper	

Method

Preheat oven to 375˚ F.

Roast red peppers in oven for 30 minutes. Remove the skin, the stem, core and seeds when cooled. Cut into 2" strips lengthwise. Set aside

In a bowl, add the thinly sliced onion, garlic cloves and 4 TBSP olive oil. Set aside

Roll out the dough on a floured board to fit a low-sided greased baking tray pinching the edges to make a border (or use the already made pizza dough and follow baking instructions)

Place the roasted red pepper strips on top of the dough all in the same direction, then add the onion, garlic and olive oil mixture
Bake at 375˚ F for 30 minutes

Cover with foil after 15 minutes so that the peppers don't dry out

Serves 4

Llentias Mallorquines
Mallorquin Lentils with Zucchini

Preparation time:	15 minutes
Cooking time:	30 minutes

Ingredients

4 ½ cups dry lentils *(for a quick but satisfying recipe, you can substitute dry lentils for canned lentils. Drain before using)*
2 large potatoes
1 medium white onion
1 large tomato
1 medium zucchini
½ cup olive oil
2 teaspoons oregano
Salt and pepper

Method

Peel and cut the potatoes, onion, zucchini and tomato into 2" squares

In a pan, add the above ingredients and cover with water

Boil for 15 minutes then add the lentils

Cover and simmer at medium heat for 30 minutes

After 20 minutes, add the olive oil

Cover and simmer for 10 additional minutes (for a total of 30 minutes)

Add water as needed to maintain a 'stew-like' consistency

Salt and pepper

Serves 4

Sopes Mallorquines
Traditional Mallorquin Vegetable 'Greixonera'

'Sopes Mallorquines' is a cross between a soup and a stew, basically made from cabbage and vegetables and served over Mallorquin country bread called pan payés seco.

Preparation time:	30 minutes
Cooking time:	25 minutes

Ingredients

8-10 slices of day-old country bread (Mallorquin pan payés seco is best for this recipe) (Melba toast may be used as a substitute)

½ cabbage	1 small cauliflower	1 large onion
2 leeks	2 garlic cloves	4 small tomatoes
1 cup fresh parsley	2 cups spinach	¼ cup olive oil
¾ cup olive oil	1 ½ teaspoons of paprika	
Salt and pepper	½ teaspoon of hot red pepper	

Method

Shred the cabbage, chop the cauliflower and leeks into small pieces (discarding any stalks), finely chop the garlic and parsley

Heat ¼ cup olive oil in a clay casserole dish ('greixonera' if you have one)

Sauté the onion, garlic, spices, add tomatoes and stir until thickened

Add the cabbage and cauliflower and cook until both have softened in texture

Add the spinach and 2 cups of boiling water

Season to taste as it should be a little hot without overpowering the flavour of the vegetables

Line individual 'greixoneras' or 'clay casserole dishes' with the 'sopes' (bread) and spoon the ingredients of the soup over the bread with only enough liquid to moisten the bread

The finished dish should be of a consistency that could be eaten with a knife and fork rather than a spoon

Serves 4

Coca de Verdura
Mallorquin Flatbread with Vegetables and Olive Oil

Preparation time:	1-hour if making the home-made pastry
Baking time:	30 minutes

Ingredients for Pastry
(You can substitute home-made pastry with store-bought pizza dough)

2 ¼ cup white flour	1 TBSP yeast	3 ½ oz olive oil
3 ½ oz lukewarm water	Pinch of salt	

Method

Dissolve the yeast with a little lukewarm water in a bowl; add the oil, rest of water and the salt. Mix in the flour a little at a time and knead as though making bread. Leave to rise covered with a clean cloth, about 1 hour in a warm place.

Ingredients for Toppings

2 cups baby spinach	2 cups baby chard	6 green onions
1 red pepper	4 garlic cloves	Salt and pepper
½ cup fresh parsley	4 TBSP olive oil	

Method

Preheat oven to 375° F. Roast red pepper in oven for 30 minutes. Peel and cut into strips lengthwise. Wash and remove stalks from chard, drain carefully, cut into pieces. Wash and chop baby spinach, parsley and green onions. Thinly slice garlic cloves. Add salt and pepper. Place all ingredients in a bowl. Set aside

Roll out the dough on a floured board to fit a low-sided greased baking tray pinching the edges to make a border (or use the already made pizza dough and follow baking instructions)

Place the roasted red pepper strips on top of the dough all in the same direction, then add the vegetable mixture. Gently add the olive oil and bake in a pre-heated 375° F oven for 30 minutes. Cover with foil after 15 minutes so that the greens don't dry out

Serves 4

Tumbet mallorqui
Aubergine and Zucchini Casserole

Preparation time:	30 minutes
Baking time:	30 minutes

Ingredients

6 medium sliced potatoes
2 cups diced red peppers
3 large chopped tomatoes
1 cup olive oil

1 medium sliced aubergine
1 medium sliced zucchini
2 garlic cloves (sliced)
Salt and pepper

Method

Preheat oven to 350˚ F.

In a pan, individually fry the potatoes first, followed by the zucchini, then the aubergine and finally the red peppers

Place the four ingredients in a 'greixonera' or 'clay casserole dish'

First, add most of the potatoes, then the zucchini, the aubergines, the peppers and a final layer of potatoes

Pour away most of the oil that is left in the frying pan and fry the garlic in the remaining oil, adding the chopped tomatoes soon after (or use the equivalent of canned tomatoes)

Cook for about seven minutes

Pour the garlic and tomatoes onto the vegetables in the 'greixonera' and bake in the oven at 350˚ F for approximately 30 minutes to finish cooking all ingredients and browning the potatoes which are on the top

Serve hot as a tapa or main dish

Salt and pepper to taste

Serves 4

Flam d'Espinacs
Mallorquin Spinach and Cheese Custard

Preparation time: 30 minutes
Baking time: 50 minutes

Ingredients

Spanish baguette, cut in thin slices (day-old bread preferable)
2 cups shredded sharp cheddar cheese
2 teaspoons Worcestershire sauce
1 teaspoon curry powder   6 eggs
2 ½ cups milk   2 cups spinach
1 ½ teaspoon dry mustard   1 teaspoon paprika
2 TBSP fresh parsley

Method

Preheat oven to 350° F.

Lightly spray a 12" ceramic dish with non-stick cooking spray

Place baguette slices in ceramic dish - enough to cover the bottom.
In a bowl, mix eggs, milk, spices, cheese, Worcestershire sauce
and spinach

Place half the mixture in the dish over the baguette slices

Place the remainder of the Spanish baguette slices
sufficiently to cover the egg mixture

Add the remaining egg mixture

Bake for 50 minutes

Allow to cool for 5 minutes
before serving

Serves 4

20

Truita de Patata
Egg and Potato Torte

I remember my Padrina having fun making this recipe. She would cover the pan with a large plate (just a little larger that the frying pan) and turn the pan upside down to transfer the tortilla onto the plate. Then she would slide the 'truita' back into the frying pan and continue to cook - all without spilling!

Preparation time: 20 minutes
Cooking time: 30 minutes

Ingredients

¼ cup olive oil
1 large onion, chopped
2 medium-sized potatoes,
   peeled and sliced
6 eggs, beaten
Salt and pepper

Method

Heat olive oil in pan

Add onion, potatoes, salt and pepper

Gently fry until beginning to turn golden

Cover the pan and cook for a further few minutes until the potato is slightly softened

Remove the onions and potatoes from the pan and drain

Put the onion and potato mixture in a bowl with the beaten eggs and gently stir

Cover the pan with a large plate (just a little larger that the frying pan) and turn the pan upside down to transfer the mixture to a large frying pan containing clean oil and cook over a low heat for 15 minutes

Serves 4

Plats de Carn

Meat Entrées

Arròs Brut
'Dirty' rice – a truly enthusiastic translation!

This is a typical Mallorquin dish. It is strong in taste and bold in flavour and any meats can be used to enhance this recipe however, my Padrina would use a mixture of chicken and pork...my great grandmother would even add escargots!

Preparation time: 15 minutes
Cooking time: 30 minutes

Ingredients

7 oz pork (chopped in medium slices)
4-6 oz olive oil
2 cups short grain rice
2 medium onions, diced
1 red bell pepper, diced
3 TBSP fresh parsley (chopped)
2 teaspoons saffron powder
2 TBSP thyme (chopped)
1 teaspoon cinnamon

7 oz chicken breast (sliced)
4 cups chicken or meat broth
2 medium tomatoes, diced
4 garlic cloves, minced
1 green pepper (garnish)
2 bay leaves
1 small dried chili, minced
2 TBSP paprika
Salt and pepper

Method

Heat olive oil in a pan and sauté the garlic, onion, bay leaves, tomatoes and red pepper

Once the onion is transparent, add the meat and cook until meat is brown. Add the paprika, chili, saffron powder and broth and let it boil

In a mortar, crush the herbs (except cinnamon) and add this to the broth then add the rice and cinnamon and cook until the rice is cooked (check after 20 minutes)

Serve with sliced green pepper

Salt and pepper to taste

Serves 4

Choriz i Ciurons
Chorizo with Chickpeas

Preparation time: 10 minutes
Cooking time: 10 minutes

Ingredients

3 medium chorizo sausages, skinned, roughly chopped.
(Any soft spicy chorizo sausage is best for this recipe, do not use dried chorizo sausage)

1 medium onion, finely chopped
2 garlic cloves, finely chopped
1 red chili, finely chopped
1 ½ cups baby spinach   2 large diced tomatoes
1 can chickpeas, drained   1 teaspoon smoked paprika
3 TBSP cilantro (fresh is best)   6 teaspoons lemon juice
2 teaspoons olive oil   4 oz chicken stock

Method

In a large saucepan, sauté the chorizo for 3-4 minutes

Add the onion, garlic and chili and cook for another
2-3 minutes, or until softened

Add paprika and fresh cilantro and stir until well mixed

Place the tomatoes, chickpeas and chicken stock in the pan and bring to a boil. Reduce heat and simmer for 5 minutes

Add the spinach and fold through. Cook for another minute to wilt the spinach, then season with lemon juice

Serves 4

Frit mallorqui
Mallorquin Fritata

| Preparation time: | 30 minutes |
| Cooking time: | 30 minutes |

Ingredients

½ lb bacon
1 ½ lbs lean pork
¼ lb pork liver
4 red peppers chopped in small squares (1" x 1")
6 large potatoes diced
1 bunch scallions
6 TBSP olive oil
2 TBSP pork drippings
2 garlic cloves (sliced thinly)
1 teaspoon chili powder
2 bay leaves
Salt and pepper

Method

Cut the bacon, pork and liver into medium size pieces and sauté until golden brown. Place them in a 'greixonera' (clay pot casserole dish). Set aside

In the same oil together with the pork drippings sauté the scallions, garlic cloves, red peppers and bay leaves. Set aside

Separately, and in clean oil, fry the diced potatoes and place them in the 'greixonera' that contains the meat

Top with the scallions, peppers, garlic and bay leaves

Return to low heat for 10 minutes and serve hot

Serves 6

Paella
Traditional Saffron Rice with Meat

Preparation time: 30 minutes
Cooking time: 30 minutes

Ingredients

2 medium pork chops (cut in small cubes)
8 oz beef steak (cut in small cubes)
1 small onion (chopped)
2 medium tomatoes (chopped)
1 red pepper (roasted)   5 TBSP olive oil
2 TBSP saffron powder   1 ¼ cup short grain rice
2 ½ cups water   Salt and pepper

Method

In a 'paellera' or large shallow frying pan, sauté the onion with the olive oil until golden brown, then add the meat

Continue cooking until the meat is seared on all sides

Add tomatoes and cook on medium heat for 10 minutes

Add the water, saffron powder and salt and pepper

Bring to a gentle boil

Add rice to the boiling water stirring once or twice only thus allowing the rice to proportionally settle

Place the roasted peppers on top of the rice (see page 6 for roasting instructions)

Cook for 15 minutes. Add additional water if necessary

Remove from heat and allow rice to settle for 5-6 minutes
before serving

Serves 6

Pilotes Mallorquines en Vi Blanc
Mallorquin Meatballs in White Wine Sauce

Preparation time:	30 minutes
Cooking time:	30 minutes

Ingredients

1 lb minced beef (regular or lean)
2 eggs (beaten)
6 TBSP chopped parsley
1 medium onion (finely chopped)
1 beef stock cube
1 ½ cups white wine
Salt and pepper

6 strips of bacon (minced)
2 garlic cloves (minced)
1 ¼ cup canned tomato
1 tsp of sugar
2 ½ cups water
½ cup flour

Method

Meat balls

In a bowl mix the meat, bacon, garlic and parsley. Season with salt and pepper

Add the beaten eggs and mix well with your hands until the mixture gets solid enough to form balls. (It will feel very wet, keep mixing and it will become firm. If it still feels too wet, add some breadcrumbs)

With floured hands roll the meat mixture to form balls. Place them on a plate with some flour. Coat the meatballs in flour and shake off the excess. Meatballs should be approximately 2 - 3 inches in diameter

Place the meatballs in a frying pan with oil and cook on all sides until golden brown. Set aside. You may want to do this in 2 batches

Wine Sauce

Sauté the onion until soft and transparent. Add the wine and cook until it has reduced by half. Add the tomatoes and a teaspoon of sugar and cook for 5 minutes. Dissolve the stock cube in the water and bring to the boil. Add the meat balls and simmer for 15 minutes. Serve hot

Makes 20 meat balls

Pollestre al Jerez
Sherry-infused Chicken in Cream Sauce

Preparation time: 30 minutes
Cooking time: 30 minutes

Ingredients

3 chicken breasts (thinly sliced)
1 cup fresh mushrooms (sliced)
1 cup fresh spinach (chopped)
1 ½ TBSP lemon juice
4 TBSP olive oil
¾ cup sweet Sherry
¾ cup whipping cream
Fresh parsley (garnish)
Salt and pepper

Method

Stir-fry the chicken in the olive oil until almost cooked

Add the mushrooms and continue to stir-fry gently for 10 minutes
Add the spinach. Pour sherry and cream into pan, bring to boil
and allow to simmer

Add the lemon juice, salt and pepper to taste and decorate
with chopped fresh parsley

Serves 4

Galletes, Cocas i Postres

Cookies, Cakes and Puddings

Coca d'Albercocs
Apricot Cake

This is truly a Mallorquin dessert delicacy. The people of Mallorca have a love of apricots and they use them in both sweet and savoury recipes.

If in a rush, white cake mix may be used (but omit the yeast).

Baking time:	30 minutes
Preparation time:	20 minutes

Ingredients

4 ½ cups apricots - peeled, rinsed, cut in half with the stones removed

2 ¼ cups flour	¼ cup white sugar
¼ cup white sugar	¼ cup icing sugar
2 eggs	1 cup olive oil
1 cup water	1 teaspoon yeast

Method

Preheat oven to 400° F.

In a mixing bowl place ¼ cup white sugar with eggs, water, yeast and oil

Beat with a wooden spoon until well mixed

Add the flour little by little until the dough is smooth and easy to manage

Leave to rise for 1 hour in a bowl covered with a clean cloth

Place the mixture in a greased flat cake tin, place the apricot halves cavity side up around the top and sprinkle with the rest of the sugar

Bake for 30 minutes

Sift icing sugar over the top before serving

Serve warm

Serves 6

Coca de Fruita de Coñac i Brandi
Cognac & Brandy Fruit Bread

Baking pan:	Pan should measure approximately 13" by 9" by 4 ½" in depth
Baking time:	40 - 45 minutes
Preparation time:	30 minutes

Ingredients

½ cup butter
1 cup flour
3 large eggs
⅓ cup dried fruit mixture
1 cup Brandy*

½ cup icing sugar
2 TBSP flour
2 teaspoons yeast (powder)
1 cup Cognac*

* Cognac and Brandy may be substituted with Marrasquino and Kirsch Liqueurs.

Method

Preheat oven to 325˚ F.

In a bowl and with a wooden spoon, mix together the icing sugar, butter and one egg. Slowly add the second egg and gently keep mixing

Add the third egg and keep mixing until batter is smooth

Add 1 cup flour and yeast and mix until a thick consistency is reached

In a small bowl, add 2 tablespoons flour. Roll the pieces of dried fruit through the flour so they separate (this will avoid the dried fruit from clumping together)

Add the 2 cups of liqueur

Bake for 40-45 minutes

Serves 6

Coca amb Ron Mallorqui
Mallorquin Rum cake

Baking time:	30 minutes
Baking pan:	12" diameter with 3" thickness
Preparation time:	Bake the cake the day before and cover until next day

Although this is a two-step recipe, it is very easy to make!

Cake Ingredients

2 eggs
1 cup white sugar
2 TBSP baking powder

½ cup milk
¼ cup icing sugar

¼ cup olive oil
1 cup flour

Rum Sauce Ingredients

1 cup water
1 cup brown sugar
1 cup dark rum
Zest of 1 lemon

Method

Preheat oven to 350° F.

In a bowl, beat the eggs then add milk and olive oil

In a separate bowl, mix all the dry ingredients (except icing sugar)
Slowly add the dry ingredients to the liquid mixture, stirring slowly

Dust the baking pan with flour and place batter in the baking pan

Bake for 30 minutes. Remove from heat and allow to cool (1 hour)
Cover and set aside

Next day - gently remove cake from baking pan and place onto a plate.
Place the cake back into the baking pan upside down (the bottom of the
cake is now the top of the cake)

Mix all rum sauce ingredients. Add the rum sauce to the cake which is
still in the baking pan

Sprinkle icing sugar and serve warm

Serves 6

Gató Mallorqui
Mallorquin Almond Cake

Preparation time: 30 minutes
Baking time: 40 minutes
Baking pan: 10 inch round baking pan

Ingredients

¾ cup ground almonds	¾ cup *caster sugar
5 large eggs	Zest of a lemon
½ teaspoon ground cinnamon	3 TBSP icing sugar

Caster sugar is preferred for this recipe. It is finer than granulated sugar but not as fine as icing sugar. Icing sugar can replace caster sugar in this recipe.

Method

Preheat oven to 400° F. When ready, reduce heat to 300° F.

Separate the eggs

Grease the cake pan with butter and lightly dust with flour

Beat sugar and egg yolks together until fluffy

Carefully, fold cinnamon, lemon zest and ground almonds into the sugar and eggs mixture

Separately, whisk egg whites until very stiff

Using a large metal spoon, stir 2 large spoonful of the egg white into the almond mixture. This will stabilize the mixture and make the next step easier. Carefully fold the remaining egg whites and pour the mixture into the prepared cake pan

Carefully smooth the surface with a spatula

Bake in reduced oven temperature for 40 minutes

Leave cake in pan to cool before serving and dust with icing sugar

Serves 6

Galletes de Maizena
Sweet Cookies

Preparation time:	20 minutes *(Refrigerate cookie mixture for 1-hour)*
Baking time:	10 - 12 minutes

Ingredients

7 TBSP unsalted butter   ¾ cup sugar
1 egg yolk   1 whole egg
Zest of half lemon
2 teaspoons baking powder
2 cups cornstarch
1 TBSP vanilla extract

Method

Preheat oven to 325° F.

Beat the butter until creamy (with a hand blender)

Add the sugar gradually, beating until mixture is light and fluffy

Add egg yolk and 1 whole egg, one at a time, beating well after each addition

Add the vanilla and lemon rind

Sift together the cornstarch and baking powder

Gradually add the dry ingredients to the butter mixture, beating until thoroughly combined

Place the cookie mixture in the refrigerator for 1-hour

Drop the batter by small spoonfuls onto well buttered baking sheets
(Leave enough space between the cookies as they will rise and spread out)

Bake for 10 - 12 minutes

Immediately remove from the baking sheets and let cool

Makes 24 cookies

Greixonera d'Ensaïmada
Ensaïmada Bread Pudding

Preparation time: 15 minutes
Baking time: 45 minutes (or until the top is golden brown)

Ingredients

2 large ensaïmadas or 2 loaves of sweet bread or raisin bread
(2 day old preferable)
4 ¼ cups milk (2%)
8 eggs
1 ½ cups white sugar
Rind of 1 lemon
2 teaspoons ground cinnamon
½ cup dark rum or brandy

Method

Preheat oven to 325° F.

Cut the ensaïmadas (or sweet bread) into small pieces and soak them in the milk

Beat 8 eggs

Mix the eggs, sugar and the soaked ensaïmadas together

Grate the rind of one lemon, and add the ground cinnamon

Mix generously

Slowly add the dark rum or brandy and continue mixing

Grease the bottom of the 'greixonera' with butter or margarine

Add the mixture and bake in the oven for 45 minutes until it sets

Serve cold

Serves 6

Postre de Poma amb Ron
Apple Rum Cake

Preparation time:	30 minutes
Baking time:	30 minutes

Ingredients

4 eggs
2 cups white flour
1 lb red apples (peeled and thinly sliced)
5 oz butter
¾ cup sugar
½ cup raisins
4 oz dark rum or brandy
Zest of 1 lemon
2 teaspoons baking powder

Method

Preheat oven to 300° F.

Place the dark rum or brandy in a bowl and add the raisins

Add the thinly sliced apples and the lemon juice

Beat the eggs and add the butter and sugar. When mixed well, add the flour and baking powder

Place mixture in a baking pan (pan to measure 4" W x 9" L x 3" H) and add the apples with the lemon juice

Bake for 30 minutes

After 20 minutes of baking, add the dark rum and raisins and continue baking for another 10 minutes

Allow to cool and serve

Serves 6

Sangria Mallorquina

This is my family's version of the popular wine and fruit drink.
My great grandfather would substitute fruits and alcohol for what
was available at the time. Often, home-made red wine was the only
alcoholic beverage available.
Later on, my grandfather would 'revise' the recipe by adding
just about any fruit you want, and if available, he would add cognac
or vodka or both!

This family recipe has maintained its authenticity throughout the
decades and is not diluted with carbonated beverages.

Preparation time: 10 minutes
Ready in 2 hours

1 lemon
1 lime
1 large orange
1 large apple
3 apricots

1 ½ cups spiced rum
¼ cup cognac
¼ cup vodka
½ cup white sugar
4 ½ cups red wine
1 cup orange juice

Preparation

Have the fruit, rum, wine, and orange juice well chilled

Slice the lemon, lime and orange into thin rounds then slice the apple
and apricots and place both in a large glass pitcher. Pour in the Rum,
Cognac, Vodka and sugar. Refrigerate for 2 hours

Adjust sweetness to taste

Serves 1-10

Pedro y Margarita

Acknowledgments

In March, 2013, after chatting with my parents about our culinary family history,
I made a decision to search for and gather our family recipes.
This was not an easy task!

Both my parents were fascinating sources of information. My search extended
to the contributions of my Tia Francisca, my Padrina, my Abuela and a wonderful
and fun-loving person and informally adopted member of our family whom
I fondly call "Lady Mimi."

I want to extend whole-hearted gratitude to everyone who shared and gathered
information in order to make this book possible. Unfortunately, some are no longer
with us. But there is an extra bright star or two in the heavens that remind us of
them. In this book, I hope their culinary and personal legacies will continue to be
enjoyed and appreciated.

"Lady Mimi" provided translations that give this book an authenticity that
I could not have achieved without her help.

Finally, I want to acknowledge and thank my father who spent many hours helping
in my time-consuming effort at gathering recipes. As always, he encouraged me
and helped me see it through to completion.

For any errors or inadequacies in this book I bear sole responsibility.

Dedication

To that very special person who taught me the ways of life,

Who takes pride in everything she does including the food

she prepares and serves her family;

Whose free spirit is defined in a few maxims, including

"Be strong and ready for today,"

"Accept people for who they are," and

"Family is the first and most important ingredient in every family recipe";

Whose grace, charm and elegance is acknowledged by all who know

her personally or by reputation; and

Whose resilient character is conditioned by gentleness,

kindness, strength and courage;

I dedicate this book to my dearly beloved Mother,

To Tia Francisca, to Padrina, to Abuela, and

To all mothers who dedicate themselves to their families.

www.ingramcontent.com/pod-product-compliance
Lightning Source LLC
Chambersburg PA
CBHW042006080426
42733CB00003B/27